H. Lazarus

METHOD FOR CLARINET

Revised by
SIMEON BELLISON

PART I   (O327)
PART II   (O328)
PART III (O329)

CARL FISCHER®
65 Bleecker Street, New York, NY 10012

ISBN 0-8258-0206-7

SIMEON BELLISON

Simeon Bellison, known in many parts of the world as a clarinet virtuoso, teacher, and arranger, was born in Moscow in 1881. His colorful and extremely active career started when, at the age of nine, he became a member of the various military bands which his father conducted. At eleven the already experienced musician entered the Moscow Imperial Conservatory of Music, from which he was graduated with honors seven years later. He taught the clarinet in several important Moscow schools, and for thirteen years was the first clarinettist of the Moscow Opera and Symphony orchestras. He toured Europe with a chamber music organization, and won the coveted position of first clarinettist in the orchestra of the St. Petersburg Imperial Opera.

In 1918, after service in World War I, Mr. Bellison organized a chamber music ensemble, "Zimro", with which he toured Siberia, China, Japan, India, the Dutch East Indies, Canada, and the United States. In 1920 he was engaged as first clarinettist of the New York Philharmonic Symphony Orchestra, which position he still holds. He has performed with almost every chamber music organization in the United States and Canada, and under most of the leading conductors of our time in Europe and America.

Settling in New York in 1920, Mr. Bellison opened his clarinet studio, which is attended by students from many parts of the world. In 1927 he organized his unique Clarinet Ensemble, which grew from eight to seventy-five players, and was active for eleven years.

Mr. Bellison has arranged over seventy pieces for clarinet and piano and for various chamber music combinations. His written works include articles on the clarinet for magazines and encyclopedias, and "Eat 'em Alive", a novel about the poor and obscure musicians of Old Russia.

For the past four years Mr. Bellison has been a member of the Board of Directors of the New York Philharmonic Symphony Society.

SIMEON BELLISON

A List of the Principal Words used in Modern Music
WITH THEIR ABBREVIATIONS AND EXPLANATIONS

A	to, in, or at; *A tempo*, in time
Accelerando (accel.)	Gradually increasing the speed
Adagio	Slow; leisurely
Ad libitum (ad lib.)	At pleasure; not in strict time
A due (à 2)	To be played by both instruments
Agitato	Restless, with agitation
Alla Marcia	In the style of a March
Allegretto	Moderately quick
Allegro	Quick and lively
Amoroso	Affectionately
Andante	In moderately slow time
Andantino	A little less slow than Andante
Appassionato	Impassioned
Arpeggio	A broken chord
Assai	Very; *Allegro assai*, very rapidly
A tempo	In the original movement
Attacca	Commence the next movement at once
Barcarolle	A Venetian boatman's song
Bis	Twice; repeat the passage
Bravura	Brilliant, bold, spirited
Brillante	Showy, sparkling, brilliant
Brio, con	With much spirit
Cadenza	A passage introduced as an embellishment
Cantabile	In a singing style
Caprice	A composition of irregular construction
Coda	A finishing movement
Col or *con*	With
Crescendo (cresc.)	Gradually louder
Da or *dal*	From
Da Capo (D.C.)	From the beginning
Dal Segno (D.S.)	From the sign
Decrescendo (decresc.)	Decreasing in strength
Diminuendo (dim.)	Gradually softer
Dolce	Softly, sweetly
Duet or *duo*	A composition for two performers
Elegante	Elegant; graceful
Energico	With energy, vigorously
Espressione, con	Expressively, with expression
Fine	The end
Forte (f)	Loud
Forte-piano (fp)	Loud and instantly soft again
Fortissimo (ff)	Very loud
Forzando (fz)	Accentuate the sound
Fuoco, con	With fire; with spirit
Giocoso	Joyously; playfully
Giusto	Exact; in strict time
Grandioso	Grand; pompous; majestic
Grave	Very slow and solemn
Grazioso	Gracefully
Largamente	Very broad in style
Larghetto	Slow, but not so slow as Largo
Largo	Broad and slow
Legato	Smoothly, the reverse of Staccato
Lento	Slow, but not as slow as Largo
L'istesso tempo	In the same time
Loco	Play as written, no longer *8va*
Ma	But; *Ma non troppo*, But not too much
Maestoso	Majestically, dignified
Marcato	Marked, With distinctness and emphasis
Meno	Less; *Meno mosso*, Less quickly
Mezzo	Moderately
Mezzo piano (mp)	Moderately soft
Moderato	Moderately; *Allegro moderato*, moderately fast
Molto	Much; very
Morendo	Gradually softer
Mosso	Moved; *Più mosso*, quicker
Obbligato	An indispensable part
Ottava (8va)	To be played an octave higher
Pause (⌒)	The sign indicating pause or finish
Perdendosi	Dying away gradually
Pesante	Heavily; with firm and vigorous execution
Piacere, a	At pleasure
Pianissimo (pp)	Very softly
Piano (p)	Softly
Più	More; *Più Allegro*, More quickly
Poco or *un poco*	A little
Poco a poco	Gradually, by degrees
Pomposo	Pompous, grand
Presto	Very quick; faster than Allegro
Rallentando (rall.)	Gradually slower
Rinforzando	With special emphasis
Ritardando (rit.)	Slackening speed
Risoluto	Resolutely; bold; energetic
Ritenuto	Retarding the time
Scherzando	Playfully; sportively
Segue	Follow on in similar style
Semplice	Simply; unaffectedly
Sensa	Without; *Senza sordino*, Without mute
Sforzando (sf)	Forcibly; with sudden emphasis
Sordino	A Mute; *Con Sordino*, With the Mute
Sostenuto	Sustained, prolonged
Spirito	Spirit; *Con Spirito*, Forcefully
Staccato	Detached, separated
Tacet	Be silent
Tempo	Movement
Tempo primo	As at first
Tenuto (ten.)	Held for the full value
Veloce	Rapid; swift; quick
Vivace	With vivacity; bright; spirited
Vivo	Lively
Volti subito (V.S.)	Turn over quickly

Part I
Contents

The contents of pages 80 to 110 serve as exercises in dynamics, expression (interpretation) and correct breathing (phrasing).

LAZARUS CLARINET METHOD
Part I
THE RUDIMENTS OF MUSIC

Before progress can be made in the study of any instrument, some knowledge of the rudiments of music is absolutely essential, so a brief explanation is given. While there are over eighty different tones used in music, there are only seven primary tones of which the others are variants or duplications lower or higher. These primary tones are named after the first seven letters of the alphabet, A, B, C, D, E, F, G, They are represented visually by note - heads (o, 𝅗𝅥, 𝅘𝅥, etc.) placed upon the *staff*.

The *Staff* consists of five parallel lines and the four intervening spaces, the lines and spaces are numbered upward. Lines  Spaces

A sign called a Clef (𝄞) is placed at the beginning of the staff to fix the position of one tone, the other tones are located in alphabetical order. In the example, the G (or Treble) Clef is placed to fix the position of the tone G on the 2nd line.

Notes too low or high in pitch to be placed on the *staff* proper are located on *Ledger Lines* (and spaces) (— = ≡) below or above the staff.

The above gives the range of notes playable on the Clarinet, the last three however being but rarely used.

DURATION OF TONES

The duration of a tone is indicated by the *form of note head* used to place it on the staff. The longest note is the Whole note o followed in order by the Half 𝅗𝅥, the Quarter 𝅘𝅥, the Eighth 𝅘𝅥𝅮, the Sixteenth 𝅘𝅥𝅯, the Thirty-second 𝅘𝅥𝅰. The shorter notes are generally connected by bars or balkens corresponding in number to the hooks,

Eighths,   *Sixteenths,*   *Thirty-Seconds.*

For detailed information in relation to the above and music in general the student is strongly advised to consult "A New Catechism of Music" (Lobe-Coon) or "The Pocket-Standard Dictionary of Music" (Oscar Coon), both published by Carl Fischer, New York.

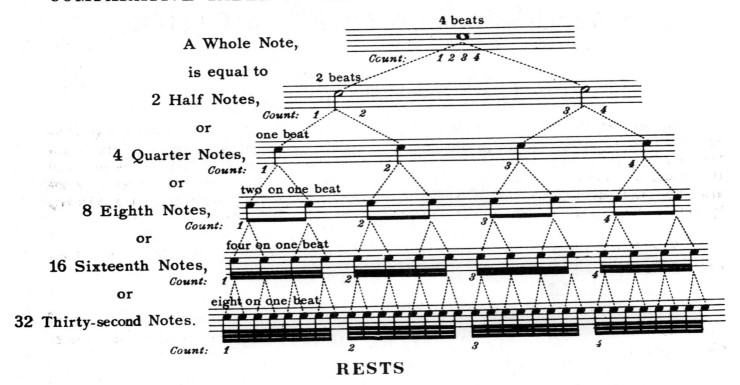

A Whole Note,

is equal to

2 Half Notes,

or

4 Quarter Notes,

or

8 Eighth Notes,

or

16 Sixteenth Notes,

or

32 Thirty-second Notes.

RESTS

The symbols indicating silence are called *rests*. For every note there is a corresponding rest having the same time value, as shown below:

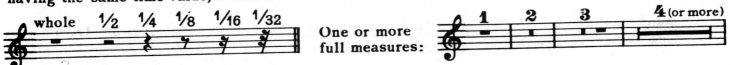

BARS

Written music is arithmetically divided into measures by bars drawn across the staff. Each measure contains the same time value. How many beats each measure shall contain is deter - mined by the time signature placed after the clef, (2/4, 3/4, 4/4, 3/8, 6/8 etc.), The top number gives the number of beats in each measure and the lower number suggests the kind of note that is to receive one beat, i.e. 2/4 means two beats to the measure, one beat on each quarter note.

The time signature most frequently used is 4/4 or common time, also marked **C**. This time signature indicates that each measure contains four quarter notes or their equivalent.

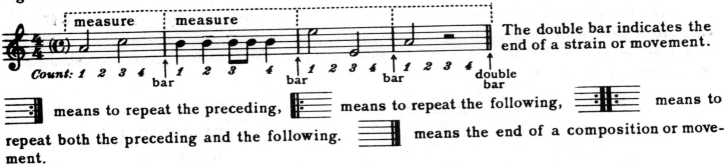

The double bar indicates the end of a strain or movement.

means to repeat the preceding, means to repeat the following, means to repeat both the preceding and the following. means the end of a composition or move- ment.

DOTS

A *dot* to the right of a note or rest increases its value by half, and each succeeding dot in- creases the value of the preceding dot by half.

TRIPLETS, SEXTUPLETS, AND ODD GROUPS

Triplets are marked by a *3* being put over a group of three notes.   Sextuplets are marked by a *6* being placed over a group of six notes. Three quarter notes marked thus ♪♪♪ must be played in the same time as two quarter notes ♪♪ not so marked; or six eighth notes ♫♫♫ in the time of four eighth notes ♫♫ not so marked. There are also groups of five ♫♫♫ seven ♫♫♫♫ and nine notes ♫♫♫♫♫ etc.

TIME SIGNATURES

In order to know how many quarter notes, eighth notes or sixteenth notes a bar contains, special figures are placed at the beginning of a movement.

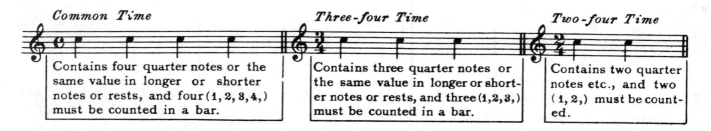

Common Time	*Three-four Time*	*Two-four Time*
Contains four quarter notes or the same value in longer or shorter notes or rests, and four (1, 2, 3, 4,) must be counted in a bar.	Contains three quarter notes or the same value in longer or shorter notes or rests, and three (1, 2, 3,) must be counted in a bar.	Contains two quarter notes etc., and two (1, 2,) must be counted.

TABLE OF TIME SIGNATURES

Simple Common Times   *Compound Common Times*   *Simple Triple Times*   *Compound Triple Times*

* When a line is drawn through the **C** thus: **₵**, which is called àlla breve, two is counted in a bar.

21443   N1033

SCALES

Scales consist of a ladder-like succession of eight or more notes progressing up or down on adjacent *Degrees* of the Staff: Each line and space is a *Degree* and they are numbered 1 to 7; the Keynote of the Scale is always the first Degree, the series is duplicated above or below.

The *tonal* distance between notes on adjacent degrees is not always the same, it may be either a *Tone* or a *Semi-tone*. The original scale is the scale of C major, sometimes called the Natural Scale (its tones are played on the white keys of the piano or organ). This Scale is shown in the example following; note carefully the order in which the Tones and Semi-tones *follow*, and which *Degrees* they *come between*. C is the Key-note on 1st degree.

SCALE OF C MAJOR
(Model for all Major Scales)

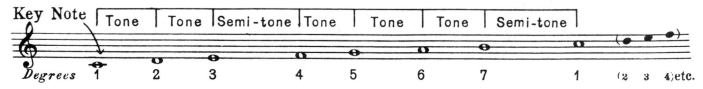

An *Interval* is the distance reckoned by Degrees between two notes, counting upward. From C to D is the Interval of a Second, C to E, a Third, and so on up to C above, which is called the Octave(8th). Going beyond this comes the Ninth, Tenth, etc. Two notes placed on same Degree form a Unison.

TABLE OF INTERVALS

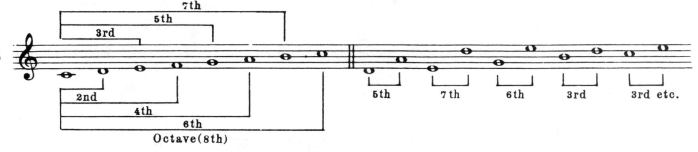

SHARPS (♯) AND FLATS (♭)

A Sharp(♯) placed before a note raises the pitch of that note one Semi-tone.
A Flat(♭) placed before a note lowers the pitch of that note one Semi-tone.

Sharps and Flats are primarily used in the formation of scales other than C Major. Any note may serve as the Key-note or 1st Degree of a new scale; but to produce the proper succession of Tones and Semi-tones as found in the model C Major Scale, certain notes are raised or lowered through the medium of Sharps or Flats.

To illustrate we will form a scale with G as the Key-note or 1st Degree.

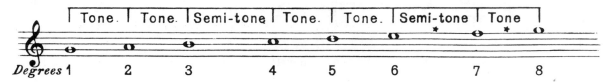

8465-99 N1033

SCALES (Continued)

In checking up the series of Tones and Semi-tones we find a Semi-tone between the 6th and 7th Degrees, and a Tone between the 7th and 8th. Both faults are corrected by adding a sharp(♯) before F, the 7th Degree.

SCALE OF G MAJOR

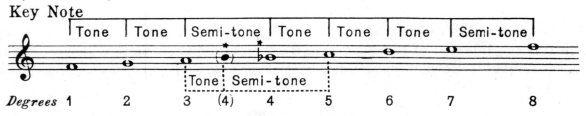

In forming certain Key-scales, flats are used to lower the pitch of one or more notes and thus correct the Tone and Semi-Tone series.

SCALE OF F MAJOR

The faulty intervals (indicated by dotted lines) are both corrected by adding a flat (♭) before B, the 4th Degree.

When used to form new scales, the sharps and flats are not added before each separate note, but are placed at the beginning of the Staff, just after the Clef, and constitute the Key-signature. For instance ♯ indicates that our original "F" (♮) has ceased to exist, we think and play only F♯; and ♭ indicates that our original B (♮) is displaced by B♭. The Key-signature may change several times during a piece, so we must always keep the signature in mind, and apply the signature sharps or flats to the proper notes.

SIGNATURES OF SHARP KEYS

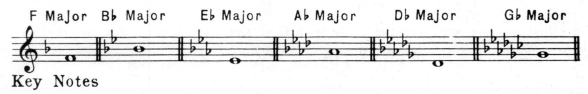

Key-Notes

SIGNATURES OF FLAT KEYS

Key Notes

Any Scale played strictly in accordance with the Key-signature is a Diatonic Scale.

THE MINOR SCALES

Every major scale has its relative minor, the root of which is to be found on the sixth degree of the major scale. Both scales bear the same signature. There are two kinds of *minor* scales, the *harmonic* and the *melodic* form.

THE MELODIC MINOR SCALE

The ascending of the melodic *minor* scale differs from the descending, the former having its sixth and seventh degree raised by *accidentals not essential to the key*. In the ascending, semitones are situated between the second and third and the seventh and eighth degrees, and in the descending between the sixth and fifth and the third and second degrees.

SCALE OF A MINOR
Without Signature; Relative to C major

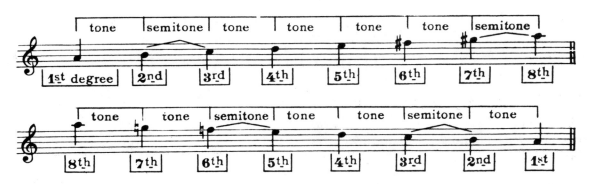

TABLE OF MINOR KEYS WITH THEIR RELATION TO MAJOR

THE HARMONIC MINOR SCALE

The Harmonic Minor Scale differs from the Melodic, as only its 7th degree is raised by an accidental, which remains, whether ascending or descending.

SCALE OF A MINOR

THE NATURAL ♮

In order to restore a note which has been raised by a sharp(♯) or lowered by a flat(♭), a *Natural*(♮) is employed which restores it to its original pitch.

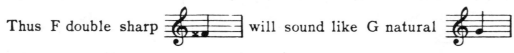

Thus F raised by a sharp is restored by the natural to its original sound.

or B flat to B natural.

THE DOUBLE SHARP ×

By prefixing a double sharp × to a note the same must be raised a whole tone.

Thus F double sharp will sound like G natural

THE DOUBLE FLAT ♭♭

A double flat ♭♭ prefixed to a note lowers the note a whole tone. Thus B♭♭

(double flat) will sound like A natural

THE PAUSE ⌢

A Pause ⌢ placed over a note, means that the note can be sustained to an indefinite length at the performer's pleasure; the counting being interrupted.

THE CHROMATIC SCALE

Consists of a succession of semitones, which, in ascending are designated by sharps, and in descending by flats.

ABBREVIATIONS

Abbreviations are employed in written music to save space or facilitate reading. Repetitions of the same note are represented as follows:

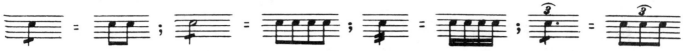

For the alternation of two notes the heavy bar is placed across or between the stems,

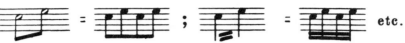 etc.

The sign ✗ is used to indicate the repetition of a group of notes or an entire measure

If placed across the bar line dividing two measures it indicates the repetition of the two measures preceding. The heavy double bar lines and dots (repeat marks) have been explained. The letters *D.C.* standing for *Da Capo* (the head or beginning) indicates play from the beginning; *D.S.* (*Dal Segno*, the sign,) indicates play from the sign 𝄋. *Fine* indicates the actual closing point of the piece.

TRANSPOSITION

Transposition consists in writing or playing music in a *new key* higher or lower than the original. The process of forming new scales (p. 10) is transposition.

In transposition on paper the signature of the new key is added at the beginning of each staff and the notes are written at an interval higher or lower; notes with *accidentals* (sharps, flats, etc., introduced here and there) must be carefully studied, but on the whole, transposition in writing is largely mechanical. Transposing simple scales in *playing* is not at all difficult once the scale formula of Tones and Semitones is fixed in mind and ear, the proper note is taken instinctively. Transposing music in general while playing is not so easy. To begin with one must be thoroughly familiar with the scales in all keys. Generally we are directed to transpose and play in a *particular* key, but often the word comes to play one, two or three (etc.) notes higher or lower and we must first find out what Key this will be. But in any case we must keep the Signature of the new Key in mind, *feel the key*, so once the transposition by degree count is made we will know simultaneously whether the new note is *sharp, flat* or *natural*. For instance, we have a passage in the Key of C which we wish to play a third higher in E (4♯), we transpose a third up and play all the "thirds up" according to the 4 sharps in the Key of E.

But suppose we wish to play it in the Key of E♭. We transpose a third up (this time beginning on E♭), and play all the "thirds up" according to the three flats in the Key of E♭.

8465-99 N1033

It is clear that there must be a tonal difference between the third from C to E and the third from E to Eb. It has been stated that the tonal difference between two notes on adjacent degrees of the staff is not always the same, likewise intervals of a third, fourth, etc., vary as to tonal content. The third from C to E is called a Major (Large) Third (2 full Tones), that from C to Eb is called a Minor (Small) Third (1 tone and a Semi-Tone). This classification of intervals belongs properly to the study of Harmony and does not necessarily concern the student now. It will be sufficient to make the transposition by intervals as directed, and remember the scale of the *new key* we are playing in.

DIFFERENT SHADES OF TONE

p means: *piano,* soft

pp means: *pianissimo,* very soft

f means: *forte,* loud

ff means: *fortissimo,* very loud

mf means: *mezzoforte,* moderately loud

cresc. or ⟨——— means *crescendo,* increasing the sound

dim. decresc. or ———⟩ means *diminuendo, decrescendo,* diminishing the sound

sf, rf or > means *sforzando, rinforzando,* sharply accentuated

fp means: *forte-piano,* loud and immediately soft again

GRACES, EMBELLISHMENTS OR ORNAMENTS OF MELODY

THE APPOGGIATURA

The appoggiatura is a grace note placed above or below a principal note. When it is placed above, it is always at the interval of either a tone or a semitone. When it is placed below the principal note it should always be at the interval of a semitone. When the appoggiatura is written so  the value of it is one half of the following note.

When crossed by a small line, thus:  its value is but a fragment of the note that follows it.

EXAMPLES

Written thus:

Played thus:

There is also a double appoggiatura which is composed of two grace notes placed: the first, one degree below the principal note, and the second, one degree above.

Written thus:

EXAMPLE.

Played thus:

THE GRUPPETTO OR TURN

Is composed of three grace notes placed between or after a principal note. The turn is **marked** thus: ∾. A small sharp placed under some of the signs thus: ∾ indicates that the lowest of the three grace notes is sharpened. Should the sharp be placed above the sign thus ∾, the upper grace note must be sharpened; or in case of a sharp above and below the sign ∾, the upper and lower grace note must be sharpened. The same rule applies to flats, only that the grace notes must be lowered half a tone in that case.

EXAMPLES

THE PASSING SHAKE (MORDENT)

The passing shake, often written thus ∿, must be played quick and round in the following manner:

THE TRILL

The shake or trill , marked thus 𝄐 consists in the alternate repetition of the note marked, with the note in the next degree above it.

EXAMPLE

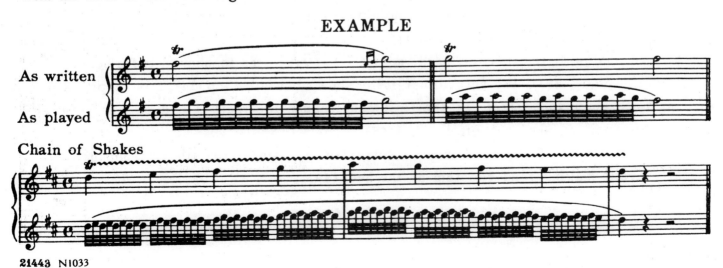

HOW TO MAKE YOUR OWN REEDS

While reeds of the best quality may now be obtained in music supply houses, some performers prefer to make their own reeds, and at least some knowledge of the process of reed-making or correcting faults is invaluable. (The figures interspersed refer to diagrams on following page.)

First cut off a piece of cane the thickness of a half dollar coin (1) and of the size of the *lay* (3) (The part of the mouthpiece where the reed is laid and held by the ligature or reed-holder).Then rub the inside part of the cane on a broad fine cut file until the surface is perfectly flat, after which it may be placed on the *lay* (3) and the screws of reed-holder tightened to ascertain if the opening (5) is correct. Holding the mouthpiece sideways against the light the opening (5) should extend downward about one inch. Remove the reed from mouthpiece and with a sharp knife trim down gradually from centre (6) to top (7) being careful not to take too much off at first as later adjustment must be allowed for. The edges should be rounded from where the cutting begins (8) and show an elongated angle from the middle. The cane should be thicker in the middle (9) than at the edges (10). The thin end of reed can be shaped with a sharp pair of scissors or a reed-cutter. If, on trial, the reed proves too hard, file off the thickness at top of reed, sloping toward edges (11). If the top is already thin enough, file off between the centre (6) and the top (7), but with great care, for should too much be taken off the tone will be spoiled. Then with a very smooth file file straight across the top of reed to a depth of $\frac{1}{8}$ of an inch downward; this will leave thin part even and al-most transparent. Again place the reed on *lay* (3) and give a side glance at the opening (5); should it be too close, loosen the top screw of reed-holder and tighten the bottom screw. Reverse the process if the opening is too large. The flat surface of the reed (2) may become warped and uneven, in which case rub carefully on the large file or on the fin-est sandpaper laid on a perfectly smooth or flat surface, preferably, plate glass.

When left on the mouth-piece for a few days, all the small faults in a reed may vanish; but the real fault may be in the mouth-piece, if located there take the mouth-piece to the maker or a repair shop for refacing.

If the reed still remains too hard, adjust it on *lay* so as to show a trifle below top of the mouth-piece, (13) if too soft adjust it to show above the top (14), this experiment will at once show the defect. In the first case reduce the reed at end of the curve (15), in the second case, cut off the top (16)

Future warping of the reed may be corrected by using large file or sandpaper, but carefully avoid making reed too thin at the heel (17).

T-126 N1033

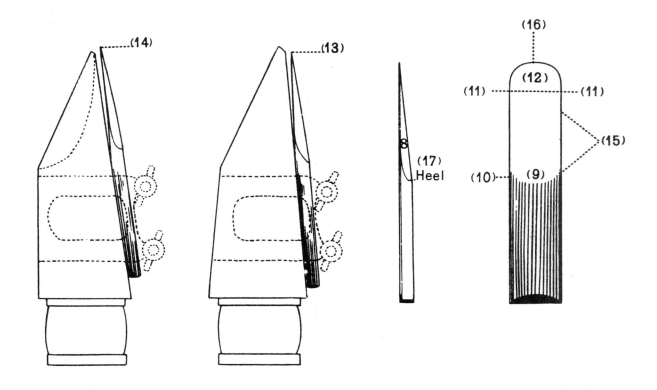

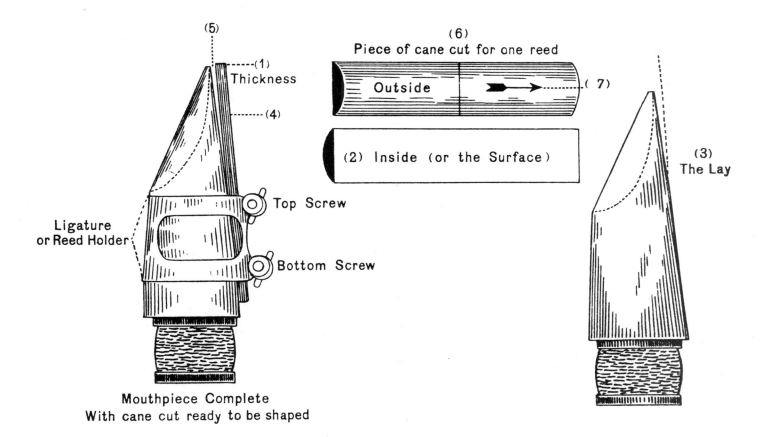

(6)
Piece of cane cut for one reed

Outside → (7)

(2) Inside (or the Surface)

(5)

(1)
Thickness

(4)

Ligature
or Reed Holder

Top Screw

Bottom Screw

Mouthpiece Complete
With cane cut ready to be shaped

(3)
The Lay

(14)

(13)

8 (17)
Heel

(16)

(12)

(11)   (11)

(15)

(10)   (9)

TO THE STUDENTS

Tutors or Methods are very essential for pupils who are learning any musical instrument, but to learn from the book without the assistance of a master is indeed tedious and very difficult.

The pupil cannot always correctly understand the contents of the book; although the Method or Tutor may be a good work, yet it may also be a little too complicated for a beginner, in such cases the pupil must hear the lessons to form some conception of the correct meaning of the text. To make him comprehend easily the master will himself use the book as a guide, and explain. _ Practical Demonstration should then accompany the explanation.

Our main object in introducing this work is to reduce the great amount of mental labour attached to long works; we are here brief, but also clear and progressive, so that in the absence of a master the beginning will be found more pleasing and far less tedious than most works already published.

———————— ∞✳∞ ————————

USEFUL INFORMATION

The use of the Clarinet in the orchestra or when accompanying the voice requires much skill. It unfortunately frequently occurs that good players are sadly neglectful, arriving in the orchestra only at the very last moment. Having immediately to commence the performance the natural result is that the instrument cannot be played in tune, being cold will cause it to be *flat* in pitch. If to remedy this evil the orchestra were to tune flat, a little time would elapse and then the Clarinet would get warm, and with the same *sharp* in pitch, consequently as before, "out of tune again!"

A conscientious Artist should not only be punctual, but arrive early enough to have time to warm, regulate and tune the instrument before the performance.

When the pitch or tuning note is required to be given by the Clarinetist, the note (A) should be sounded *on the A Clarinet*; the reason for it is that when the tuning note (A. Concert pitch) is sounded on the Bb Clarinet it is fingered B♮, the same B♮ is a sensitive note which never sounds in unison with the "A" of the Orchestra. To sound the "A" on the "C" Clarinet would produce a like result to the Bb, hence always select the A Clarinet to sound the *A Concert pitch*. give C upon the A Clarinet, which will give the sound of A.

When performing before an audience, bear a calm appearance, emit the sounds without showing externally the difficulties that have to be overcome; it will greatly impress those around you with the apparent facility of your execution. On the other hand; it would offer the company some temptation to laugh if you were to move your head, balance the body, raise the shoulders as a mark of expression, fill up your cheeks with wind.

———————— ∞✳∞ ————————

8465-99 N1033

THE CLARINET

The Clarinet is the most useful and important of all the wood-wind instruments, and is indispensable to both band and orchestra. The Clarinet is constructed on the principle of the single reed, which was originally applied to several crude instruments known as Shawm, Schalm, Chalumeau. In 1690 John Christopher Denner of Nuremberg, began experimenting and evolved the instrument (though still imperfect) which, under the hands of later inventors has become the Clarinet of today; a well nigh perfect instrument of wonderfully expressive and controllable tone, wide range and almost unlimited capabilities. The full compass is as given below, but the extreme upper notes are at best, hazardous, and G is about the limit for practical purposes.

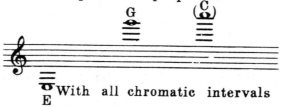

With all chromatic intervals

THE DIFFERENT PITCHED CLARINETS

The C Clarinet is a non-transposing instrument; its "C" sounding in unison with "C" played on the Violin, makes it possible to play from same music as written for Violin, Piano or Voice.

The E♭ Clarinet is the highest pitched Clarinet in general use, its "C" sounding the E♭ above on Violin or C Clarinet. It is necessary in the military band and is sometimes introduced in the orchestra.

The B♭ Clarinet is the most universally used in band and orchestra; it is pitched a full tone below the C Clarinet; its "C" sounding B♭ on that instrument or the Violin.

The A Clarinet is used only in the orchestra to play such music as is written in sharp keys for the Violin, etc. Its "C" sounds "A" on Violin or C Clarinet.

The E♭ Alto Clarinet is now generally used in the band and sometimes in the orchestra, its C sounds E♭ (a major sixth below on Violin or C Clarinet.)

The B♭ Bass Clarinet is a necessary part of every well-balanced band and is generally found in large orchestras. It sounds a major ninth below the written note as written in the Treble Clef; that is, when reading from same notes as ordinary B♭ Clarinet, the sounds are an octave lower. While formerly written for in the Bass clef, the Treble is used entirely now.

Most Clarinets are made of five pieces; the mouth-piece, the tuning barrel, the top joint with three holes in front covered by the index, middle and third fingers of the left hand.

8465—99 N1033

The hole at the back is covered by the thumb, which has an immediate control over the octave B♭ key above. (Extend the little finger so as to reach keys N° 1 and 2 at command.) The next is the bottom joint, held by the right hand. The index, medium and 3ʳᵈ fingers cover the three holes in front of this joint. The thumb supports the Clarinet by means of a metal rest fixed at the back. (Extend the little finger so as to reach keys N° 3 and 4 at command.) Lastly the bell.

As for any other instruments, the attitude of the player should be free and easy, and without stiffness; the head and body upright. The mouth-piece must be placed, with the reed under, in the mouth, about half an inch between the lips, taking care that the teeth do not bite the reed nor even touch it. The hands holding their respective joints should not be stiff; the arms and elbows resting naturally upon the side of the ribs; The distance of the bell from body should not be more than nine or ten inches. Hold your clarinet steady, and avoid swinging yourself.

ON THE EMBOUCHURE, SOUND AND WIND

The embouchure is the soul of the Clarinet and like the Violin with bad or good strings on, will give bad or good tone; the difference being that on the Violin it is the material quality of the strings that gives the tone, while on the Clarinet it is the result of the player's own feeling and taste in blowing, which requires great delicacy.

The sound is produced by the wind, which causes the thin part of the reed to beat rapidly against the table or lay of the mouth-piece. If a rough blow of wind is introduced in the instrument, the reed will either stick against the mouthpiece and stop the sound, or produce a fearful noise by no means musical; if the wind is too weak no power will be obtained. The mouth-piece being placed as shown in Art. III, inhale a sufficient quantity of air and blow moderately and steadily, taking care not to let the air escape by the sides of the mouth. Do not breathe through the instrument, but by the sides of the mouth. The breathing must be effected when there is a rest in music, or at the end of a phrase, and without any apparent contortion. Avoid, when blowing into your instrument, puffing the cheeks out, or moving the jaws or head; the body should be immobile.

The lungs, the tongue and lightness of fingers combined with good expression are the principal subjects in action.

ON THE TONGUING

Unlike the Flute, Cornet and Flageolet, the Clarinet is not associated with this style; therefore **the triple** tongueing must be left to those named instruments. The best that can be done is a sort of soft tremolo in the low register, as placed with discernment by some composers in adagio and religious music, in imitation of the waving of a deep toned reed in an organ. The tongueing must be practised very slowly, and gradually increased in rapidity, until it can be done smoothly and evenly.

ON THE LIPS

The lips have great action in the performance. The pupil will soon find in his first practice that his lips will fail him; he should rest for a while, during which time he can make his fingers practice and run evenly over the scale, then resume again. The notes of the upper register are obtained by pinching the lips; those of the low register require less pressure.

THE MOUTHPIECE AND REED

The mouthpiece should be carefully considered before proceeding with practice; the surface of the table or *lay* where the reed is placed must be perfectly true and flat. Constant moisture is liable to warp the surface of the *lay*, and the best materials to guard against this are Ebonite or Crystal (which is rather brittle). In selecting reeds, strike a medium between hard and soft, but only in the course of practice will the student discover the type of reed best suited to him. The mouthpiece is placed in the mouth with reed below, resting upon the under lip. The teeth as previously stated should never touch the reed; as a most acute and painful tone results thereby.

TYPES OF CLARINETS

At the present time there are two methods of fingering, known as the Albert and the Boehm system. Each one is subject to modifications; that is to say, while the principle remains the same they may differ regarding the number of keys.

The early Clarinets were on the ordinary Albert System and in their original form were exceedingly primitive and unsatisfactory; but eventually developed into the ordinary 13 key and 2 ring Clarinet. Thereafter new keys were gradually added, such as the patent C♯ Key and B♭ or E♭ Key for trilling, which will be found described on the chart for 15 Key Clarinet.

Years of experimenting on the addition of new keys resulted in the development of an entire new system of fingering, called the "Boehm", which was originally devised by Theobald Boehm to perfect the intonation on the flute and later applied to other wood - wind instruments. This system is universally used abroad, especially in France and it is only a question of time when the same condition will prevail in this country.

The Boehm Clarinet is much better in tune and has an even scale, in other words the quality of tone is alike throughout the different registers. This system of fingering is more practical and better adapted to the overcoming of technical difficulties than the ordinary Albert Clarinet.*)

It requires but a small amount of practice on the part of an Albert system player in order to acquire a practical knowledge of the new fingering. A special chart of the Boehm Clarinet will be found on the reverse side of the Albert system chart.

ADVICE TO THE STUDENT

Like all worth while musical instruments the Clarinet demands application and intelligent practice on the part of the student before any results are obtained. First of all study tone production, starting on middle C. Begin very softly, swell the tone gradually to *ff* and let it die away as the breath is expended.

*) The Carl Fischer Perfected Clarinet is the most highly improved Albert System instrument, possessing 16 keys, 6 rings, and roller keys for little fingers of both hands; also articulated G♯ key, fork B♭ fingering, and extra E♭ key for little finger of left hand. A special chart is issued for this system.

8465-99 N1033

This should not be done in a ridiculous way of sentimental emphasis, but in a moderate and regulated way, without jerks of sounds, or sudden transition of p to f. Attack the note with firmness and finish it without hesitation; that is to say, do not keep blowing it until your wind is totally exhausted.

Practise two hours, one at a time every day for a week, and devote another hour, if you have no knowledge of music, to reading and learning by heart the rudiments of music (shown at the beginning of this work); without which knowledge, you will be stopped every moment for lack of understanding the many signs and marks used in music. The second week and following ones practise three or four hours; the lips by that time will become less liable to fatigue.

TRANSPOSITION FOR CLARINETS OF DIFFERENT PITCHES

In making any transposition, select the Clarinet that will provide the easiest Key In the example below the C Clarinet and Violin are in Unison in Key of C. If the player had to choose between a B♭ and A Clarinet to play the same notes, he would naturally take the B♭, playing a tone higher in D (2♯), as against a tone and one half higher in E♭ (3♭) for the A Clarinet.

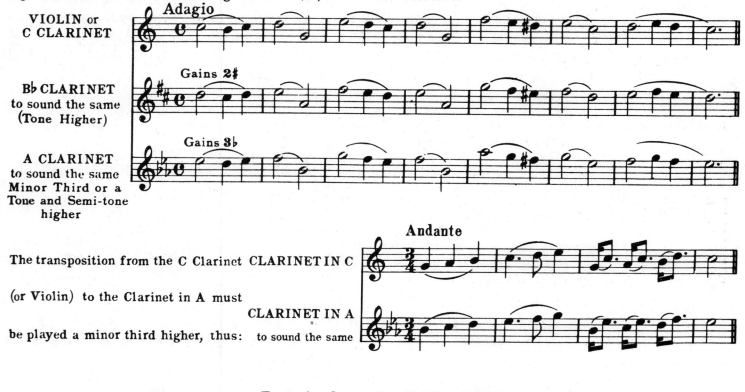

The transposition from the C Clarinet (or Violin) to the Clarinet in A must be played a minor third higher, thus:

From the Opera: LA GAZZA LADRA

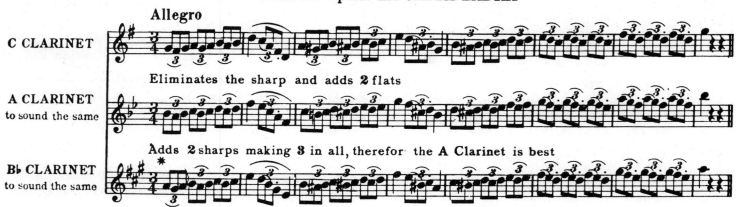

* This is (*very difficult*) for those who have not the patent C♯ Key, but can be played with more facility on the Boehm Clarinet.

AMERICA or GOD SAVE THE KING

It may be useful here to call attention to the different tonal qualities of the Clarinet. It has four distinct kinds of tones.

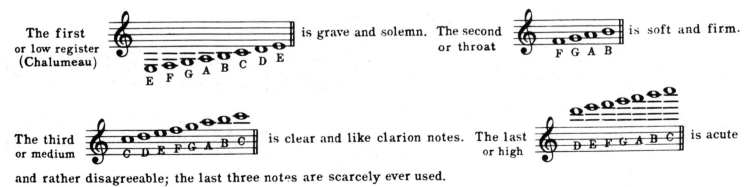

and rather disagreeable; the last three notes are scarcely ever used.

It will be understood by the above differences in the general tone of the Clarinet that the professional has to deal with the difficulty of studying each of these particular **registers so as to arrive at a perfect homogeneity of tone throughout the instrument.**

Table of Trills
for
Albert System Clarinet

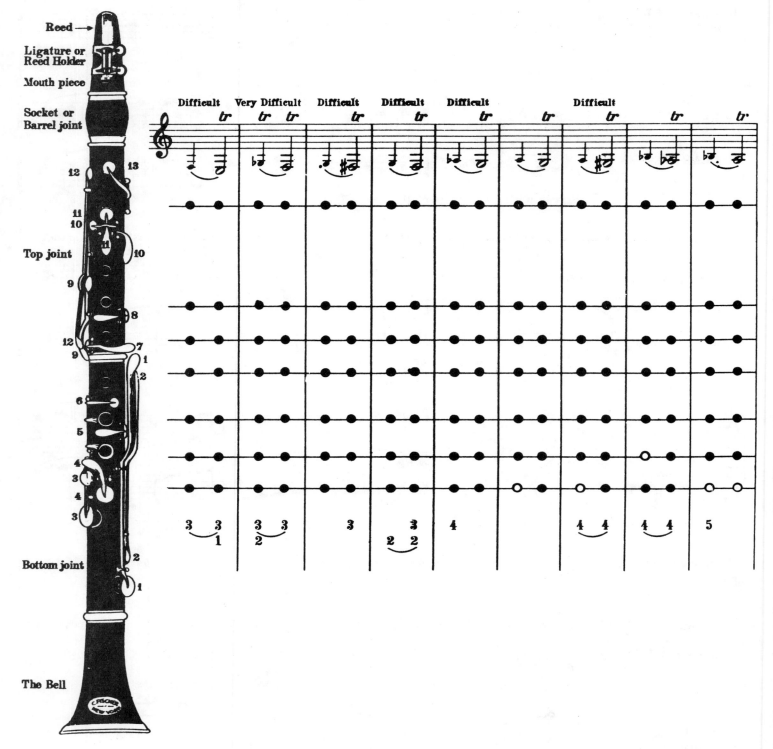

25

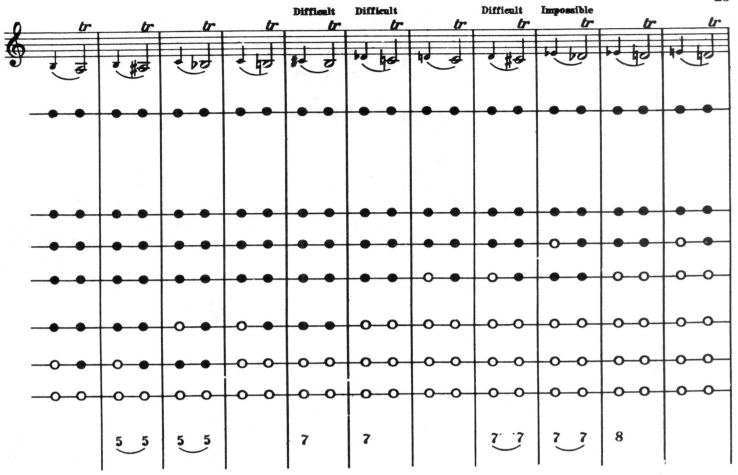

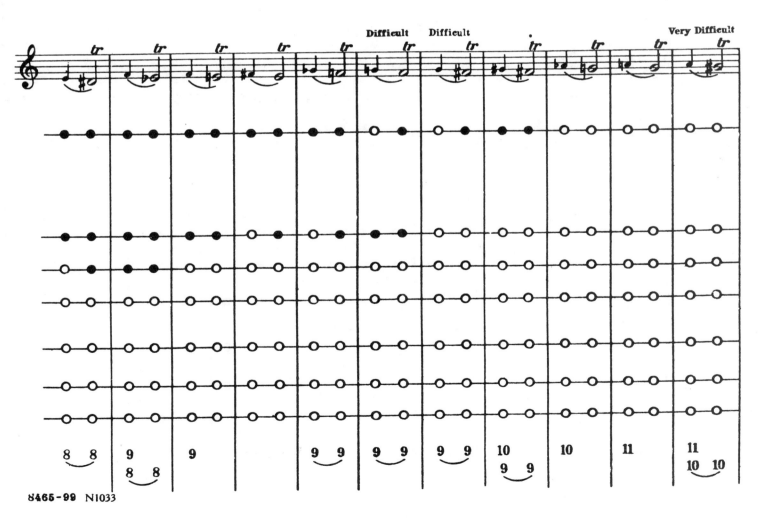

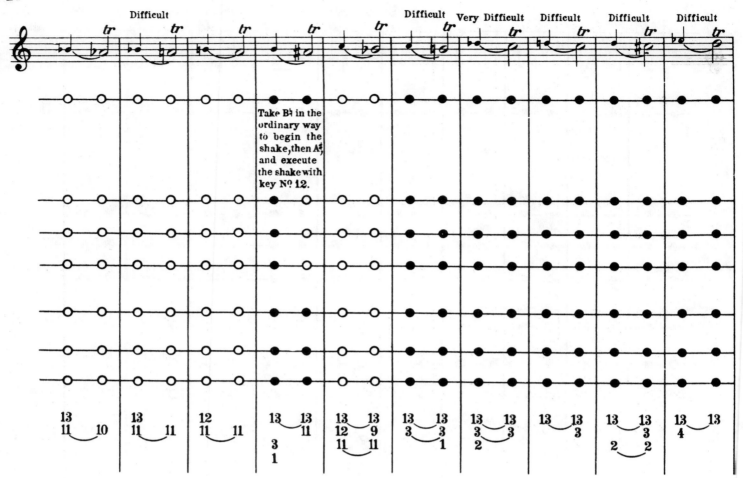

Take B♮ in the ordinary way to begin the shake, then A♯, and execute the shake with key № 12.

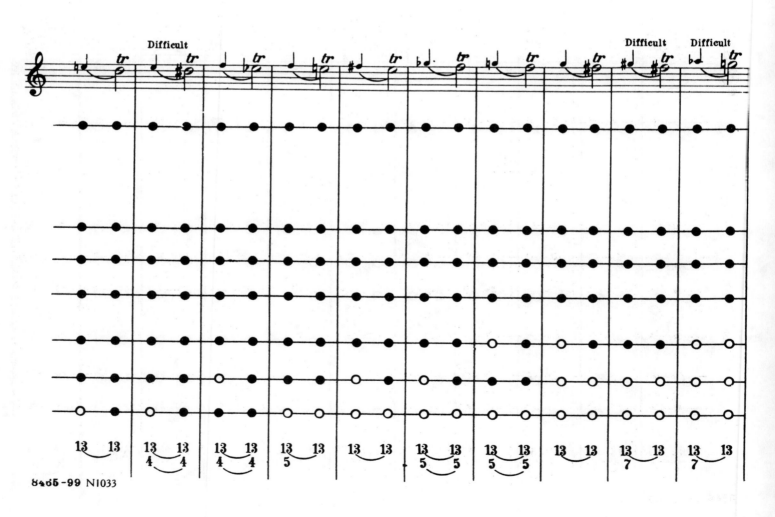

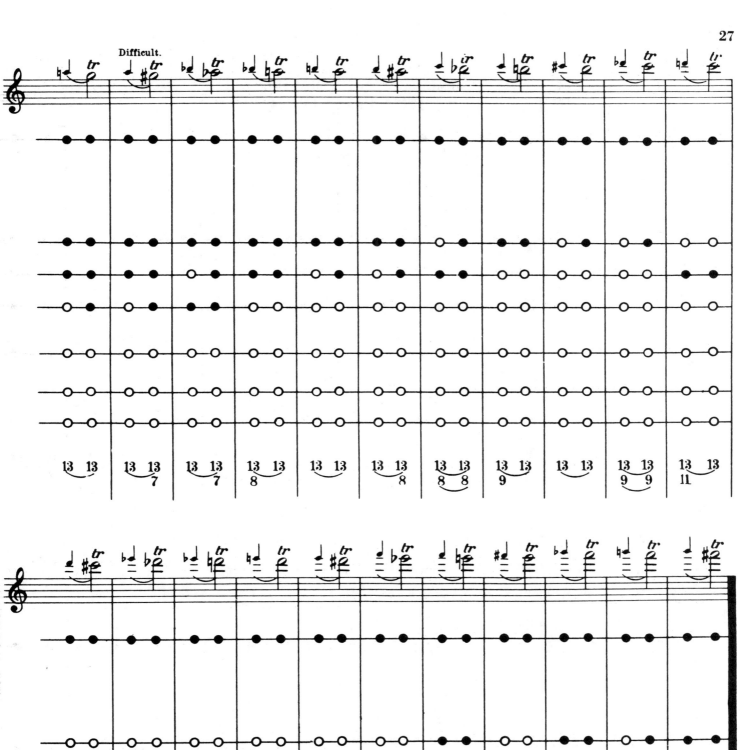

SPECIAL NOTICE

ON THE

BOEHM SYSTEM CLARINET

This new and beautiful system, justly approved and adopted in the French army and at the Conservatoire of Paris, is perfectly in tune, and possesses above ordinary models an invaluable purity and evenness of tone throughout the instrument.

Its splendid but simple mechanism of keys opens one hole for each note.

The imperfect notes, the cross fingerings and difficulties hitherto experienced in the ordinary system completely disappear in the Boehm system. The best proof of the superiority of this new system is that it has been applied to all the wind instruments, even to the Flageolet.

On its appearance it was rejected, as generally are all new improvements; by the artistes, who, being illdisposed against the little trouble in the change of fingering, left it abandoned during some years. But a few artistes, being struck by its real superiority, undertook to popularise it; and now almost every French Clarinet player performs upon it and a great many Belgian, English, German and Italian artistes use it, and it is rapidly taking the place of the ordinary or Albert system in this country.

To render familiar the use of the rings and new fingering we give (page 112.) some examples of passages which cannot be effected upon the ordinary system and which become easy upon the Boehm system, also some special exercises and studies will be found (page 113) for those professionals who will wish to change for the best.

A beginner on the Boehm Clarinet, after having carefully studied the scale, can use this book from beginning to end without paying attention to the ordinary system.

————∞✱∞————

THE EDITOR

8466-99 N1033

FIRST LESSONS

PRELIMINARY EXERCISES

It seems natural to begin with the scales and from the low notes; but experience has clearly proved that these low notes cannot be obtained until the pupil has acquired the habit of carefully stopping the holes and is a little accustomed to the use of the mouth-piece.

Carefully study Exercise Nº 1 as preliminary practise in reading (do not play); then begin actual playing with Nº 2, repeating each note many times and studying the tone. Hold the mouth-piece naturally between the lips; the teeth must never come in contact with the reed.

TO LEARN THE NATURAL NOTES OF THE CLARINET

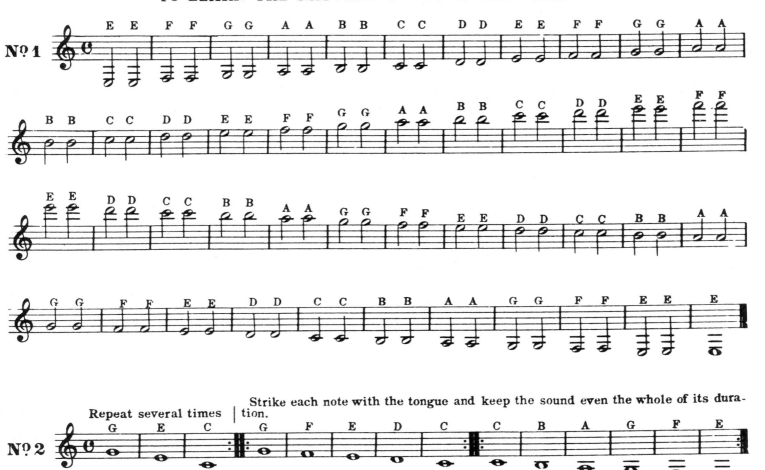

LESSON TO LEARN THE NOTES OF THE BOTTOM JOINT

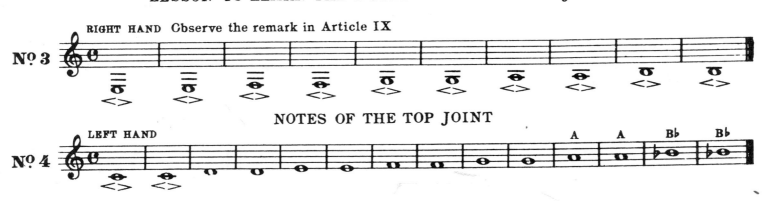

NOTES OF THE TOP JOINT

8466-99 N1033

EXERCISES ON LESSONS № 3 and 4

DIATONIC SCALE UP TO SECOND C (Clarion)

EXERCISES UP TO THIRD E

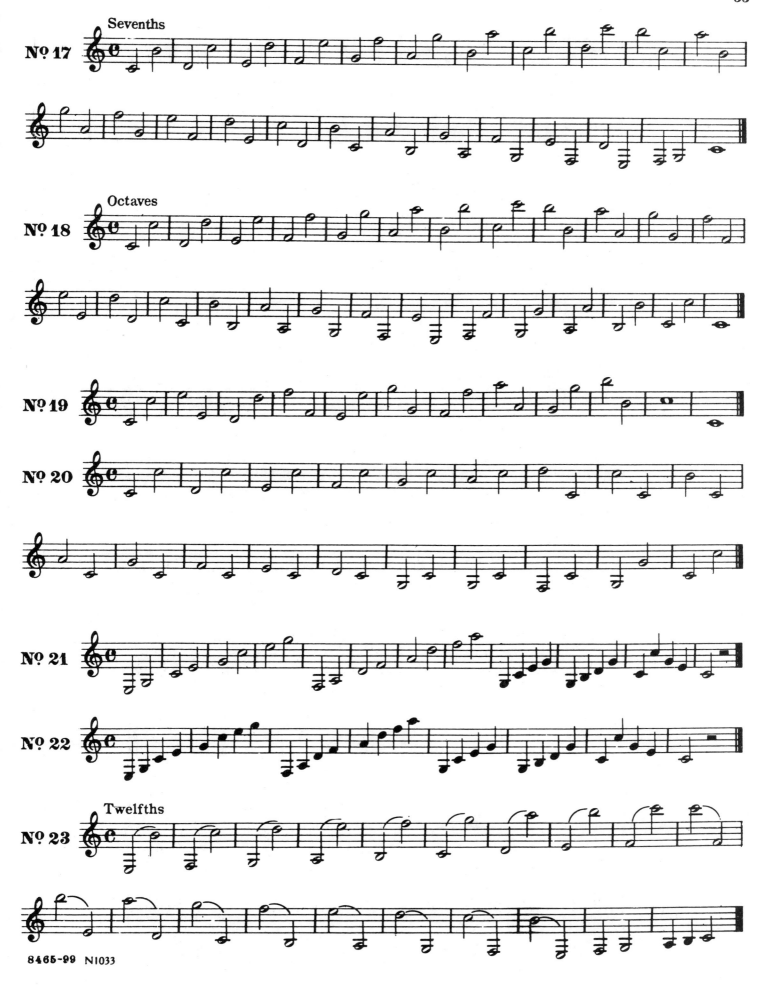

Nᵒ 24

Nᵒ 25

ON THE SLUR

The slur ⌢ placed over two or more notes on *different* degrees indicates that the first note only is tongued, the other notes following smoothly under uninterrupted wind pressure *(legato)*.

The tie ⌢ is the same sign placed over two notes on the *same* degree, binding 1st to 2nd.

Example

Tongue   T......   T....................   T....................

EXERCISES ON THE 1st REGISTER

Nᵒ 1

EXERCISES ON THE 2nd REGISTER

EXERCISES ON THE 3rd REGISTER

LESSONS IN DUET TO LEARN TO PLAY IN TIME

marcato

*) Use the fork fingering where this sign ʌ appears over the F.

8465-99 N1033

Nº 10

VARIETY IN THE SLUR

Give a little more accent (without the tongue) to the first note of each small slur.

1st Example
Slurred slur

Strike firm the first note of the slur with the tongue and the other notes very softly without interrupting the e-mission of the wind.

2nd Example
Pointed slur or mezzo Staccato

3rd Example
Pointed slur

4th Example

5th Example

8465-99 N1033

RHYTHM

The time in each bar should be decidedly marked from the beginning of a melody, so that the rhythm may be well understood.

SYNCOPATION

Syncopation consists in introducing notes on an **unaccented** beat or off the beat entirely and carrying these notes past the next accent or beat.

In Ex.1 the natural measure accents are **1** and **3**, but the syncopated note comes on *2* and carries over *3*.

ON THE POINTED NOTE

This is a light stroke of the tongue, a little more accented than for the ordinary note.

2nd Example

3rd Example

10 STUDIES RESUMING THE PRECEDING ARTICULATIONS

Two notes slurred and two pointed

No 1

Three notes slurred and one pointed

No 2

Notes slurred two by two

No 3

Strike each note carefully

No 4

No 5

FIVE EASY DUETS

Nº 2

Nº 3

Nº 4

Nº 5

ON THE STACCATO

The notes having this long dash ˈ above them, are accented with a sharper strike of the tongue called staccato.

Example

As written

As played

Detached or Broken spaces

Allegro assai

10 LITTLE PROGRESSIVE DUETS

H. Lazarus
Revised by Simeon Bellison

№ 5

№ 6

No 9

No 10

Staccato

ON THE EMPHASIS (PORTAMENTO)

The sign ⟨ ⟩ which is frequently met with in music adds to the expression of the style, if executed with taste.

Attack softly the note (undermarked) with this sign, gradually increasing and diminishing the power of the sound, with evenness in the emission of the wind.

1st Example

From forte to piano

2nd Example

In the following example each note is attacked with vigour and dropped at the end of its duration. This accent is of very good effect when properly placed; it is called *Rinforzando*.

3rd Example

The small sign > or < over or under one note is to be observed only for that note.

4th Example

PLAIN SOUNDS (FRENCH *SONS FILÉS*)

A sound leading from one note to another from soft to forte but not so strongly marked as in the Emphasis.

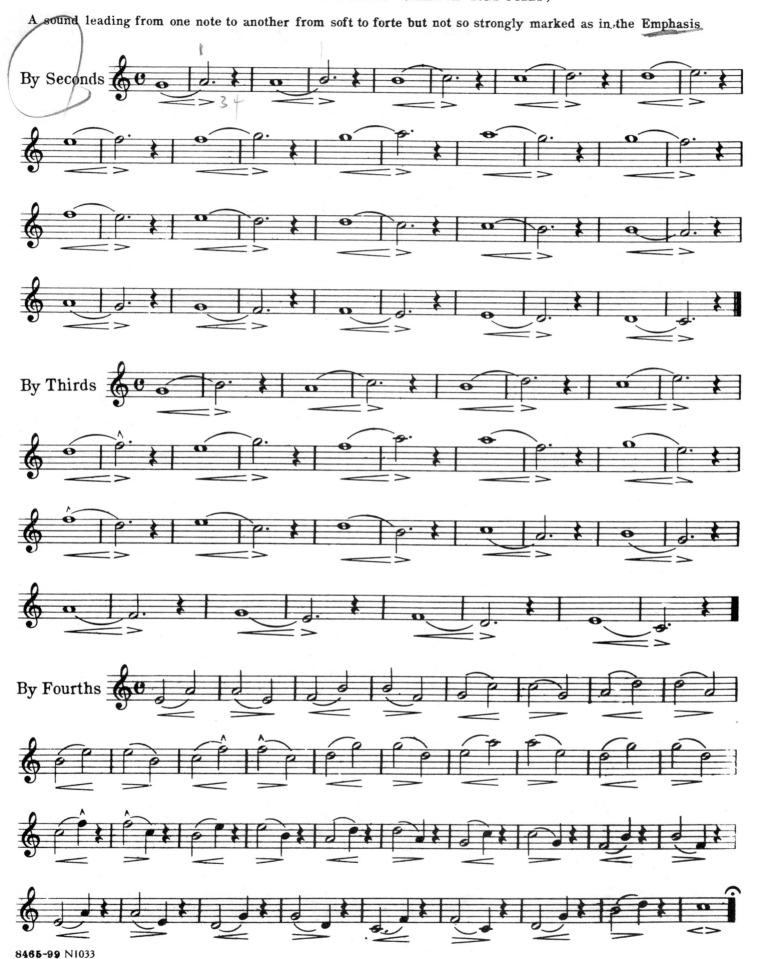

By Fifths

By Sixths

5ths and 6ths — Lento

4 in the Bar

12 LESSONS TO LEARN THE TIME

8465-99 N1033

PRACTICAL STUDIES ON THE LOWER NOTES

Fifty Progressive Duets
for two Clarinets

Revised by Simeon Bellison

Exercise in Whole notes for sustaining the tones

Joseph Küffner, Op.80

Measure of 2 beats

1.

Mixed with Half notes

2.

Half and Quarter notes

3.

The rest on the first Beat

4.

The rest on the 2nd Quarter Beat

5.

The rest on the 3rd Quarter Beat

6.

The rest at the end of the bar

7.

Exercise on the slur

8.

3200-26 N1033

To detach the first note, and slur the three others

9.

To slur the three first notes and detach the fourth

10.

To slur the notes in counter-time
(A form of Syncopation)

Half notes (2 Quarters) in contrast to four Eighth notes (2 Quarters)

Same as Nº 12 with Eighth notes coming first

13.

Detach first Eighth note and slur the three others

14.

Slur the first three notes and detach the fourth

15.

Syncopation in Halves and Quarter notes
(Syncopation in both parts)

Syncopation in Quarter and Eighth notes
Upper part syncopated, lower part even time

G major.

The same syncopations in both parts

To tie the notes from one bar to another

Syncopations and ties from one bar to the other

Syncopation in triple time
(Tieing 3rd beat to 1st beat of following measure)

Mixed Syncopation in Eighths and Quarter notes in Triple time

To acquire the unequal parts of 6/8 time

Tonguing of the same note

The half-staccato

To detach all the notes

D.S. al Fine

Strongly detached notes

Tempo di Minuetto

27.

Fine

TRIO

D.S. al Fine

Dotted Quarter notes

28.

Dotted Eighth notes

Tempo di Marcia

29.

The same Exercise

Tempo di marcia

Triplets on the second Quarter note

Triplets on the first Quarter note

Triplets on the first and second Quarter note

33.

Fine

D.S. al Fine

Eighth Rest

Sixteenth Rest in ⅜ time

The slur over half notes

SICILIANO
Exercise on Grace notes, introducing the key of C minor

37.

Key of B flat

38.

The Trill (Shake)

39.

Short Trill

40.

41. Moderato

Key of D minor and D major

42. Andantino

Major

Fine.

Rondo form

Rondo

46.

Theme and Variations. Andantino

47.

Fine

D.S.al Fine

Polonaise (Bolero)

50.

TRIO

Fine

D. S. al Fine

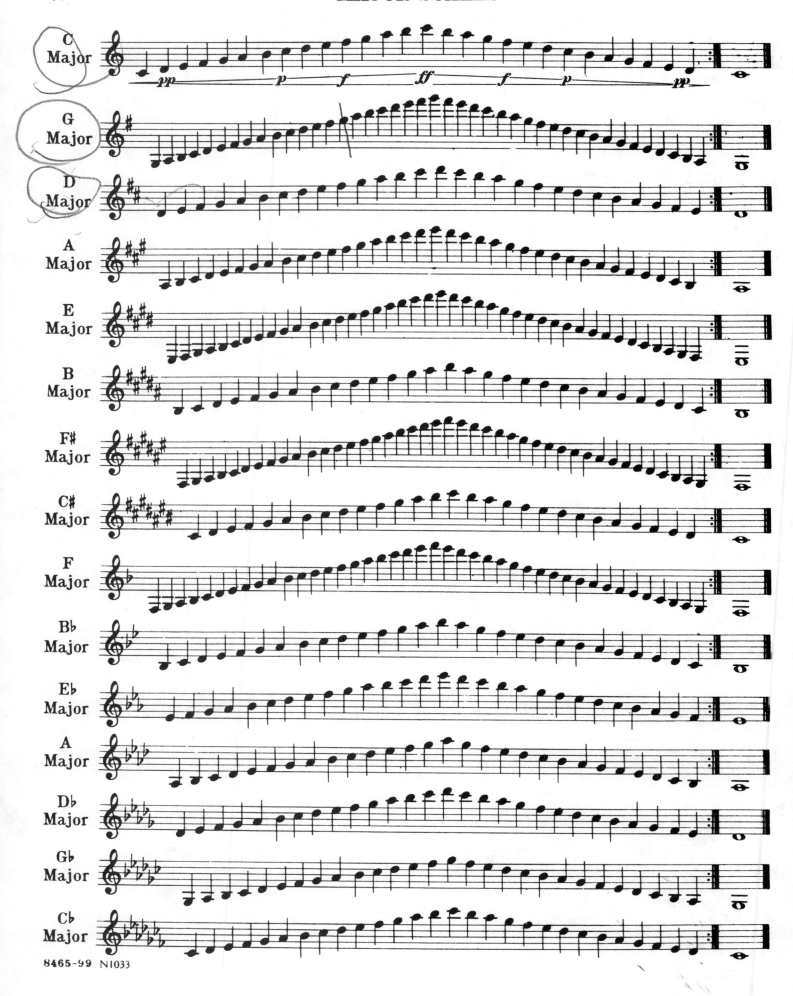

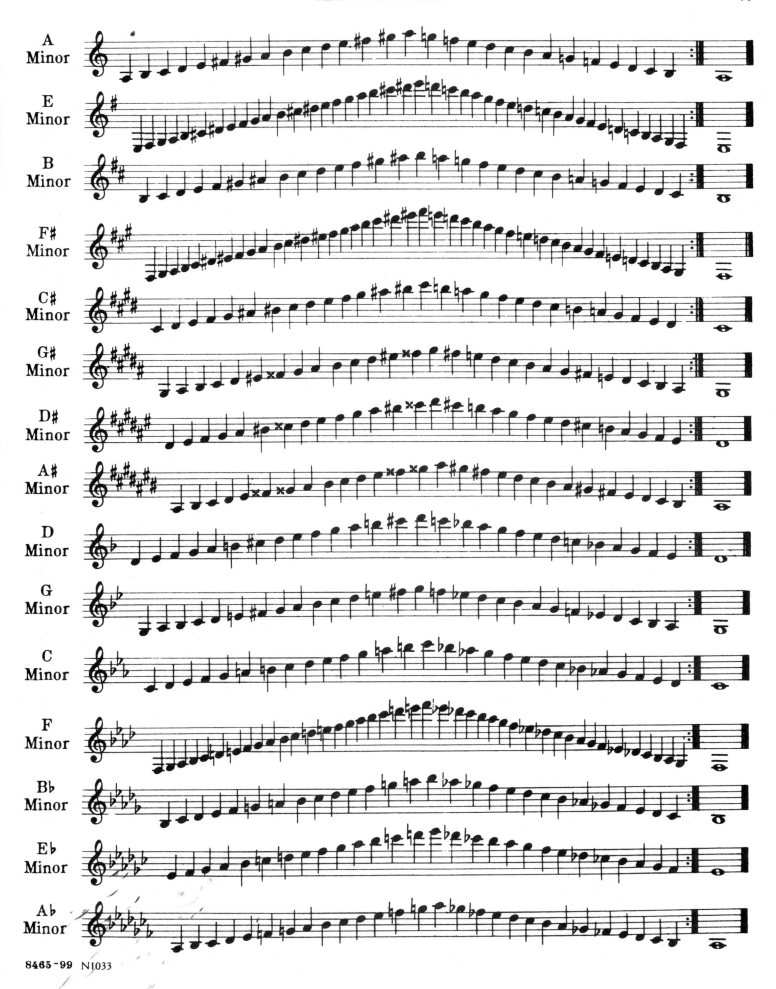

Carry Me Back to Old Virginny

JAMES BLAND
Arr. by H. R. Kent

Swing Low, Sweet Chariot

Negro Spiritual
Arr. by H. R. Kent

29123-162   N975   N1033

20 EASY LITTLE TUNES

H. Lazarus
Revised by Simeon Bellison

82

15 LITTLE OPERATIC MELODIES

From ANNA BOLENA and GAZZA LADRA

H. Lazarus
Revised by Simeon Bellison

88

8465-99 N1033

90

8465-99 N1033

20 EASY AND PROGRESSIVE DUETS

H. LAZARUS
Revised by Simeon Bellison

GRÉTRY

March

Nº 6

Allegretto

Nº 7

REDOWA

Nº 8

1st time   2nd time

Moderato

Nº 11

TYROLIENNE

Nº 12

GALOP.

GERMAN THEME

EIGHT FANTASIAS

FANTASIA ON DON GIOVANNI

H. Lazarus
Revised by Simeon Bellison
MOZART

GERMAN AIR

SWISS AIR

GERMAN AIR

BOLERO

Tempo di Bolero

FANTASIA ON NORMA

BOEHM CLARINET

Examples of passages impossible upon the ordinary clarinet system
and which become easy upon the Boehm system.

Twelve Exercises and Studies

To enable the learner to become familiar with
the extra rings and special fingerings of the

BOEHM CLARINET

by HENRY LAZARUS
Revised by Simeon Bellison

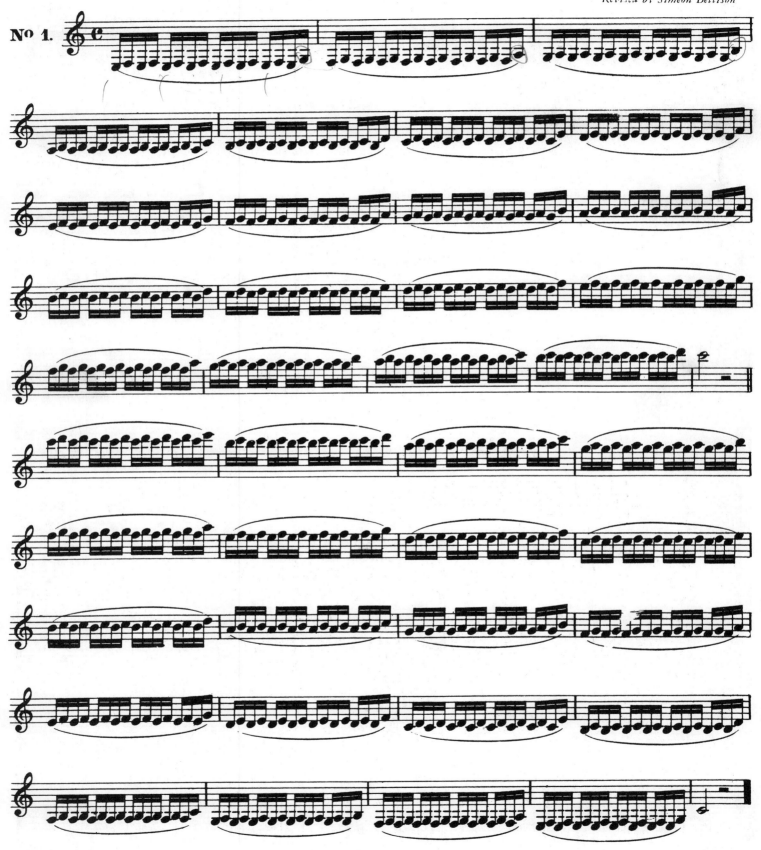

No 12

BOEHM CLARINET

TABLE OF THE SHAKES AND THEIR FINGERINGS

The fingers of both hands will be classified thus: the thumb, 1st, 2nd, 3rd and little fingers.

The numerical order of the holes starts from the mouth-piece, viz. 1st, 2nd, 3rd holes left hand and 1st, 2nd, 3rd holes right hand. The hole at the back of top joint will be called thumb hole.

Abbreviations. K. means key, R.H. Right Hand, L.H. Left hand.

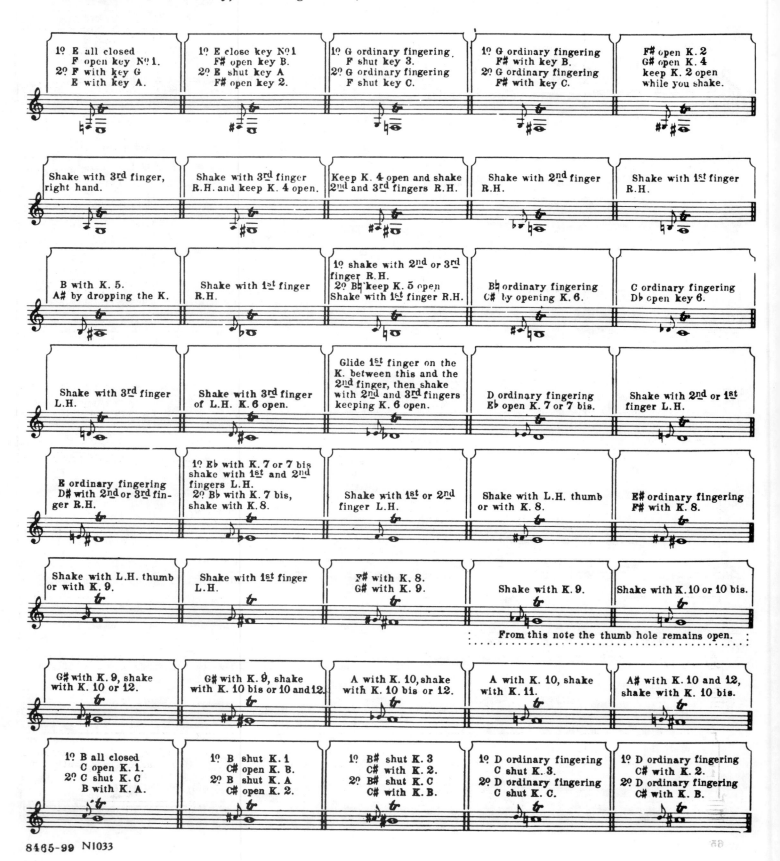

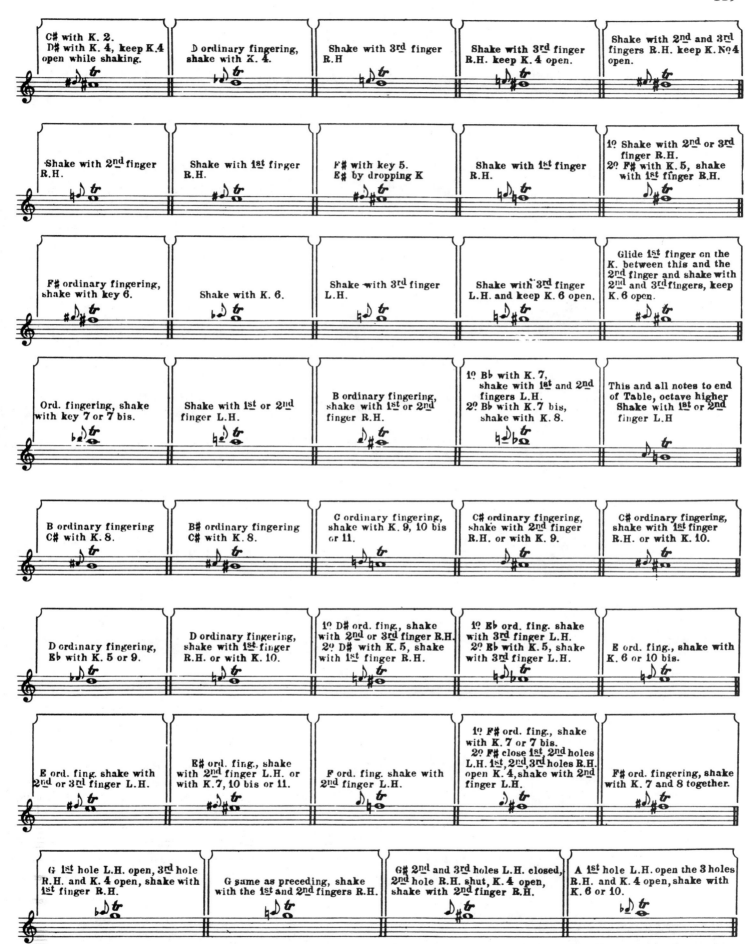

119

8465-99 N1033

EXERCISES ON THE CHORDS
MEDIUM

DOMINANT SEVENTH

DIMINISHED SEVENTH

FIFTEEN STUDIES IN THE MEDIUM REGISTER

Revised by Simeon Bellison

Henry Lazarus

Moderato

2.

Moderato

3.

Allegro non troppo

7.

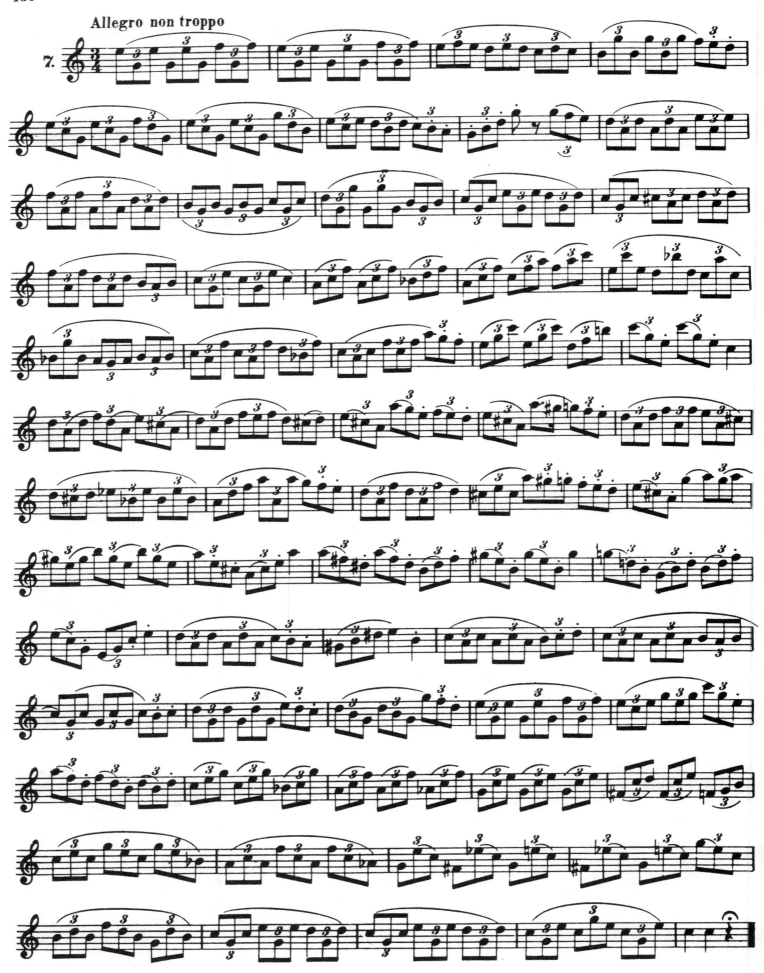

Allegro vivace

8.

Adagio

10.

AIR WITH VARIATIONS
FROM DONIZETTI'S ELISIRE D'AMORE

Revised by Simeon Bellison

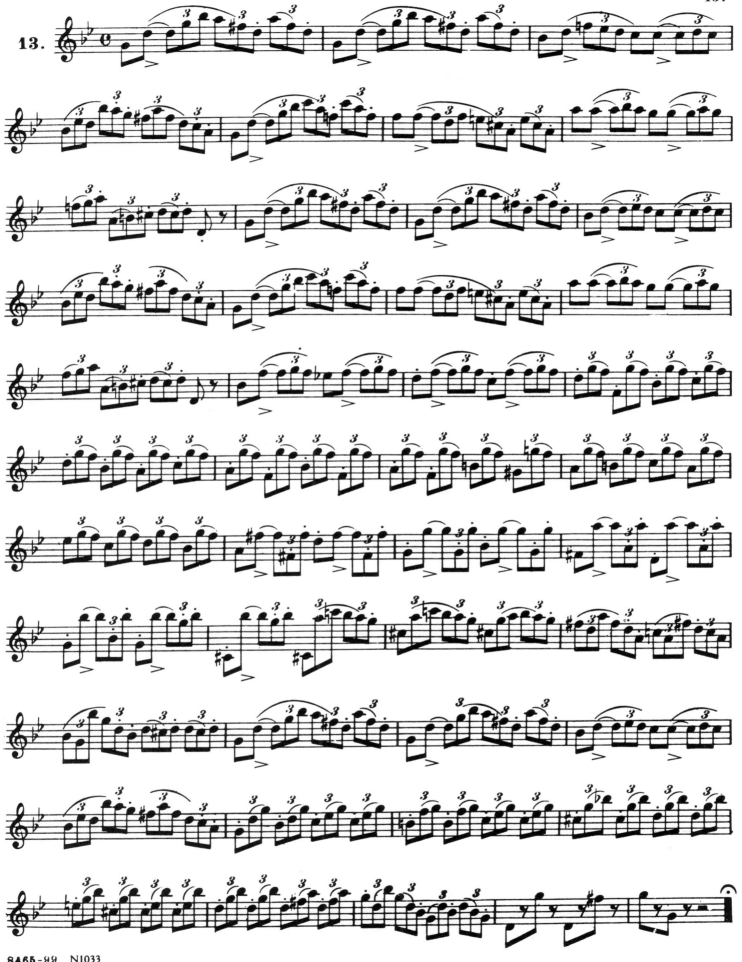

Allegro

14.

Vivo

15.

PRACTICE PLANNER

Date	Page	Goals/Comments	Remarks
Date	Page		

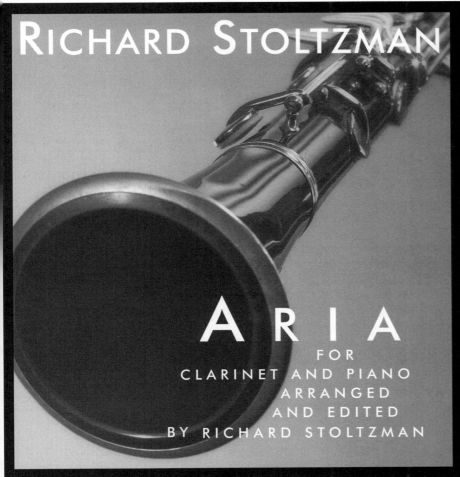

RICHARD STOLTZMAN

ARIA
FOR CLARINET AND PIANO
ARRANGED AND EDITED
BY RICHARD STOLTZMAN

Major-league clarinetist, Richard Stoltzman developed his interest in the operatic repertoire through his wife's passion for Opera. This collection, which provides clarinet and piano versions of celebrated arias from Opera and Operetta, derives from his sensational BMG classics CD, Aria. The 18 selections in the handsome print folio include popular arias from Roméo et Juliet (Gounod), La bohéme and Gianni Schicchi (Puccini), La traviata, Il Trovatore and La Forza del destino (Verdi), a suite of tunes from Carmen (Bizet) and three selections from Porgy and Bess (Gershwin).

Clarinet and Piano - 136 pp.
Clarinet Solo Part - 48 pp.
O5387

The best-known American clarinetist of the present day, Richard Stoltzman, has collected twenty four of his favorite short pieces and encores for this fine collection. Drawn from many of his popular recordings, The Richard Stoltzman Songbook draws on the variety of styles that Stoltzman has made his own.

BY POPULAR DEMAND
THE Richard Stoltzman
SONGBOOK
For Clarinet and Piano

HIGHLIGHTS INCLUDE:

Popular & Jazz Songs by:
• Bill Douglas
• Duke Ellington
• Richard Rogers
• Cole Porter

Classical Selections by:
• J.S. Bach
• W.A. Mozart
• Gabriel Fauré
• Camille Saint-Saëns

Special Gershwin items:
• Jan Gach's transcription of "Three Preludes for Piano"
• A medley of "Fascinatin' Rhythm," "Embraceable You" and "I Got Rhythm"

Plus:
• Stoltzman's own transcription of Lukas Foss' "Three American Pieces" and his arrangement of "Amazing Grace"

Piano Score – 176 pgs,
Clarinet part – 64pgs
ATF141

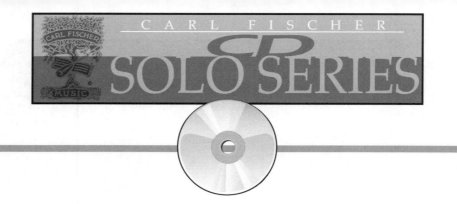

Favorite Solos with Piano Accompaniments on CD

The Carl Fischer CD Solo Series is designed to help all levels of instrumental soloists improve their performances by making practice time more productive with the included "live" piano accompaniment.

The CD contains a beautifully recorded piano accompaniment performed by Melody Lord who has years of experience accompanying soloist of all ability levels.

The CD Solo Series is an invaluable teaching tool and is presented in 3 graded levels: Beginning (Gr. 2), Intermediate (Gr. 3) and Advanced (Gr. 4-5).

As an added bonus, the faster pieces in the Beginning Level have a second track with the piano accompaniment at a rehearsal tempo to assist in the preparation of the piece.

Works for Clarinet and Piano

In the Carl Fischer CD Solo Series

Beginning level

W2624	Arioso — Largo from *Concerto for Harpsichord and String Orchestra*	Johann Sebastian Bach
W2628	Gigue	Arcangelo Corelli
W2629	Gymnopédie No. 2 from *Trois Gymnopédies*	Erik Satie
W2630	Musical Moment from *6 Moments Musicaux*	Franz Schubert
W2579	Tambourin	François Joseph Gossec
W2627	Träumerei from *Scenes from Childhood* ("Kinderscenen")	Robert Schumann

Intermediate Level

W2582	Allegretto	Benjamin Godard, Op. 116, No. 1
W2584	Berceuse	Gabriel Fauré, Op. 16
W2583	Entr'acte from *Carmen*	Georges Bizet
W2581	Giga from *Sonata in F Major*	George Frideric Handel, Op. 1, No. 1
W2585	Sicilienne from *Pelléas et Mélisande*	Gabriel Fauré
W2625	Siciliano from *Sonata No. 2 in E♭ Major*	Johann Sebastian Bach
W2626	Sonata in F Major	Benedetto Marcello

Advanced Level

W2586	Concertino	Carl Maria von Weber, Op. 26
W2587	Concerto No. 1 in F minor for B♭ Clarinet and Piano	Carl Maria von Weber, Op. 73
W2588	Grand Duo Concertant	Carl Maria von Weber, Op. 120, No. 1
W2632	Introduction, Theme and Variations from *Sehnsuchts-Walzer* by Franz Schubert	Ferdinand David
W2590	Sonata in E♭ Major, Op. 120, No. 2	Johannes Brahms, Op. 120, No. 2
W2589	Sonata in F minor for Clarinet and Piano	Johannes Brahms, Op. 120, No. 1
W2631	Theme and Variations Fourth Movement from *Quintet for Clarinet and Strings*	Wolfgang Amadeus Mozart, K. 581